BENEFITS OF AI DIGITAL SKILLS IN THE MODERN WORLD

Dr. Albert Chukwunyere Ndeze

GLOBAL
PUBLISHING
SOLUTIONS

AI DIGITAL SKILLS IN THE MODERN WORLD by Dr. Albert Chukwunyere Ndeze
Published by Global Publishing Solutions, LLC
923 Fieldside Drive
Matteson, Illinois 60443
www.globalpublishingsolutions.com

Library of Congress Control Number:
2026944031
International Standard Book Number:
979-8-9958936-8-4
E-book International Standard Book Number:
979-8-9958936-9-1

Printed in the United States of America

DEDICATION

To the learners who never stop asking questions. To the educators who light the path forward. To the innovators who dare to imagine a better world. And to every reader who believes that technology should serve humanity—this book is for you.

AI DIGITAL SKILLS IN THE MODERN WORLD

Dr. Albert Chukwunyere Ndeze

CONTENTS

FOREWORD

We are living through a transformation as profound as the invention of electricity or the birth of the internet. Artificial Intelligence is the defining force of our age, and digital skills are the new literacy. This book arrives at a crucial moment: when individuals, businesses, and societies must decide whether to fear AI or to harness it. It offers clarity, encouragement, and a roadmap for thriving in an AI-powered world. For anyone seeking to understand not just what AI is, but what it means for their future, this book is both timely and essential.

PREFACE

When I began exploring the role of AI in everyday life, one truth became clear: AI is no longer optional. It is everywhere, quietly influencing the way we live, work, and learn. Yet many people still feel uncertain about how to engage with it. This book was written to bridge that gap. It is not a technical manual—it is a guide to understanding the benefits of AI digital skills in practical, human terms. My hope is that readers will walk away not only informed but also inspired to embrace AI as a partner in their journey.

ACKNOWLEDGMENTS

This work is the result of inspiration, collaboration, and support from many voices.

To the educators who continue to champion digital literacy.

To the innovators and entrepreneurs who show us what is possible when AI meets human creativity.

To the communities worldwide embracing technology as a tool for inclusion and empowerment.

And to the readers, your curiosity and courage to learn are the true driving forces behind this book.

Thank you for being part of this journey into the benefits of AI digital skills for the modern world.

CHAPTER-OPENING QUOTES

Introduction: *"AI is not the future—it is the present unfolding before us."*

Chapter 1: Understanding AI in Everyday Life *"The most powerful technologies are those we no longer notice."*

Chapter 2: Core AI Digital Skills *"Digital skills are the new literacy of the modern age."*

Chapter 3: Benefits for Individuals *"Mastering AI is not about machines—it's about unlocking human potential."*

Chapter 4: Benefits for Businesses *"Innovation belongs to organizations that learn faster than their competitors."*

Chapter 5: Benefits for Society *"When societies embrace AI, progress becomes collective."*

Chapter 6: The Future of AI Skills *"The future is not written—it is coded, and we are the authors."*

Conclusion: *"The question is not whether AI will change the world, but whether we will shape that change."*

CHAPTER 1

UNDERSTANDING AI IN EVERYDAY LIFE

Artificial Intelligence (AI) is no longer confined to research labs or futuristic movies—it has become woven into the fabric of daily living. From the moment we wake up to the time we go to bed, AI quietly shapes our routines, decisions, and interactions. To appreciate the benefits of AI digital skills, we must first understand how deeply embedded AI already is in modern life.

AI in Our Devices

Smartphones: Predictive text, voice assistants like Siri or Google Assistant, and facial recognition are all powered by AI. These tools make communication faster and security stronger.

Smart Homes: AI-driven thermostats, lighting systems, and voice-controlled hubs (like Alexa) learn our preferences and optimize comfort while saving energy.

Wearables: Fitness trackers use AI to interpret heart rate, sleep patterns, and activity levels, offering personalized health insights.

AI in Consumer Choices

Shopping: Recommendation engines on platforms like Amazon or Netflix analyze browsing history and suggest products or shows tailored to individual tastes.

Entertainment: AI curates playlists on Spotify, generates movie suggestions, and even powers video game opponents that adapt to player behavior.

Social Media: Algorithms decide which posts we see, shaping our digital social interactions and influencing trends.

AI in Workplaces

Productivity Tools: AI enhances email filtering, calendar scheduling, and document drafting, freeing professionals to focus on higher-value tasks.

Recruitment: AI scans, resumes, matches candidates to job descriptions, and reduces bias in hiring processes.

Decision-Making: Businesses use AI analytics to forecast demand, optimize supply chains, and personalize customer experiences.

AI in Infrastructure

Transportation: Navigation apps like Google Maps use AI to predict traffic and suggest optimal routes. Autonomous vehicles are testing the limits of AI in mobility.

Healthcare Systems: AI assists in diagnosing diseases, predicting outbreaks, and managing patient records efficiently.

Public Services: Governments deploy AI for fraud detection, resource allocation, and smart city planning.

The Invisible Role of AI

What makes AI fascinating is its invisibility. Most people don't consciously notice when AI is at work—it simply feels like technology "just works." But behind the scenes, algorithms are constantly learning, adapting, and improving outcomes. Recognizing this hidden presence is the first step toward appreciating why AI digital skills are essential for navigating the modern world.

CHAPTER 2

CORE AI DIGITAL SKILLS

If AI is the engine driving the modern world, then digital skills are the keys that allow individuals to harness their power. Just as literacy was once the gateway to opportunity, AI digital skills are now the foundation for thriving in the 21st century. These skills go beyond technical expertise—they represent the ability to interact, adapt, and innovate with intelligent systems.

Data Literacy

Definition: The ability to read, interpret, and question data.

Why it matters: AI thrives on data. Understanding how information is collected, processed, and visualized empowers individuals to make informed decisions rather than blindly trusting algorithms.

Example: A marketing professional who can analyze customer data with AI tools can identify trends and predict consumer behavior more effectively.

Prompt Engineering

Definition: Crafting clear, precise instructions for AI systems to generate useful outputs.

Why it matters: AI tools like chatbots and generative models respond differently depending on how they are guided. Knowing how to "speak AI" is becoming a critical communication skill.

Example: A student using an AI tutor can get better explanations by asking structured questions rather than vague ones.

Automation Basics

Definition: Using AI-powered tools to streamline repetitive tasks.

Why it matters: Automation frees up time for creativity, strategy, and human connection.

Example: A small business owner can automate invoice processing, appointment scheduling, and customer follow-ups, reducing workload and errors.

Ethical Awareness

Definition: Understanding the social, cultural, and moral implications of AI use.

Why it matters: AI can amplify biases, invade privacy, or be misused. Ethical awareness ensures responsible adoption.

Example: A recruiter using AI screening tools must be aware of potential bias in algorithms and ensure fairness in hiring.

Adaptability and Lifelong Learning

Definition: The ability to continuously learn new tools and adapt to evolving AI technologies.

Why it matters: AI is not static; skills that are relevant today may evolve tomorrow.

Example: A teacher who learns to integrate AI-powered learning platforms stays ahead in delivering personalized education.

Collaboration with AI

Definition: Treating AI as a partner rather than a replacement.

Why it matters: The most powerful outcomes emerge when humans and AI work together, combining creativity with computational power.

Example: Journalists use AI to analyze large datasets for investigative reporting, while still applying human judgment to craft compelling narratives.

The Skillset as a Whole

These core AI digital skills form a toolkit for navigating the modern world. They are not reserved for tech experts; they are becoming essential for students, professionals, entrepreneurs, and everyday citizens. Mastering them means not just surviving in an AI-driven society, but thriving.

CHAPTER 3

BENEFITS FOR INDIVIDUALS

Artificial Intelligence is not just reshaping industries—it is transforming personal lives. For individuals, mastering AI digital skills opens doors to new opportunities, enhances creativity, and provides tools for lifelong growth. This chapter explores how AI empowers people on a personal level.

Career Advancement and Employability

Competitive Edge: Employers increasingly value candidates who can leverage AI tools for analysis, automation, and innovation.

New Roles: AI literacy prepares individuals for emerging careers such as data analysts, AI trainers, and digital ethicists.

Example: A job seeker who understands how to use AI-powered resume builders and interview simulators can stand out in a crowded market.

Personal Productivity

Efficiency: AI assistants help manage schedules, filter emails, and prioritize tasks.

Focus: By automating repetitive work, individuals can dedicate more time to strategic thinking and creative pursuits.

Example: A freelancer using AI project management tools can juggle multiple clients without missing deadlines.

Creativity and Innovation

Idea Generation: AI can spark inspiration by suggesting designs, writing prompts, or musical compositions.

Collaboration: Creative professionals use AI as a partner to refine their work, not replace it.

Example: Writers use generative AI to overcome writer's block, while artists experiment with AI-driven design platforms.

Lifelong Learning

Personalized Education: AI tutors adapt lessons to individual learning styles and pace.

Accessibility: Language translation and adaptive learning tools make knowledge more inclusive.

Example: A student struggling with math can receive tailored explanations from an AI tutor, improving confidence and performance.

Accessibility and Inclusion

Assistive Technologies: AI enhances accessibility for people with disabilities through speech recognition, text-to-speech, and predictive interfaces.

Equal Opportunities: Digital skills ensure that individuals with diverse needs can participate fully in education and work.

Example: A visually impaired professional can use AI-powered screen readers to navigate complex documents.

Personal Growth and Empowerment

Decision-Making: AI provides insights into health, finance, and lifestyle choices, helping individuals make smarter decisions.

Confidence: Mastering AI tools builds digital confidence, reducing fear of technology.

Example: A person using AI-driven fitness apps can track progress, set realistic goals, and maintain motivation.

The Individual Advantage

For individuals, AI digital skills are more than technical know-how—they are enablers of empowerment. They help people work smarter, learn faster, and live more creatively. In a world where technology evolves daily, those who embrace AI skills will not just adapt, they will thrive.

CHAPTER 4

BENEFITS FOR BUSINESSES

Artificial Intelligence is not just a tool for individuals—it is a strategic asset for organizations. Companies that embrace AI digital skills gain efficiency, unlock innovation, and strengthen their competitive edge in the global marketplace. This chapter explores how businesses benefit from cultivating AI literacy across their workforce.

Efficiency and Cost Reduction

Automation of Routine Tasks: AI streamlines repetitive processes such as data entry, customer support, and inventory management.

Operational Savings: By reducing human error and optimizing workflows, businesses save time and resources.

Example: A logistics company using AI-powered route optimization can cut fuel costs and improve delivery times.

Enhanced Customer Experience

Personalization: AI analyzes customer behavior to deliver tailored recommendations, offers, and services.

24/7 Support: Chatbots and virtual assistants provide instant responses, improving satisfaction and loyalty.

Example: An e-commerce platform using AI-driven product suggestions increases sales while making shopping more enjoyable for customers.

Innovation Through Insights

Data-Driven Decisions: AI uncovers patterns in large datasets that humans might miss, guiding smarter strategies.

Product Development: Businesses use AI to predict market trends and design products that meet emerging needs.

Example: A healthcare startup leveraging AI analytics can identify gaps in patient care and develop new solutions faster.

Global Competitiveness

Scalability: AI enables businesses to expand operations without proportional increases in cost.

Agility: Companies with AI skills adapt quickly to market changes, staying ahead of competitors.

Example: A multinational corporation using AI for supply chain management can respond to disruptions more effectively than rivals.

Risk Management and Security

Fraud Detection: AI systems monitor transactions in real time to flag suspicious activity.

Cybersecurity: AI enhances defense against evolving digital threats.

Example: Financial institutions use AI to detect anomalies in customer accounts, preventing fraud before it escalates.

The Business Advantage

For businesses, AI digital skills are not optional—they are essential. Organizations that invest in AI literacy empower employees to innovate, improve customer relationships, and operate more efficiently. In a competitive global economy, AI skills are the difference between leading and lagging.

CHAPTER 5

BENEFITS FOR SOCIETY

Artificial Intelligence is not only transforming individual lives and businesses—it is reshaping society at large. When communities embrace AI digital skills, the benefits ripple outward, improving healthcare, education, sustainability, and public services. This chapter highlights how AI contributes to collective progress.

AI in Healthcare

Early Diagnosis: AI systems analyze medical images and patient data to detect diseases faster and more accurately.

Personalized Treatment: Algorithms tailor therapies to individual patients, improving outcomes.

Public Health: AI predicts outbreaks and supports resource allocation during crises.

Example: AI-driven diagnostic tools help doctors identify cancer at earlier stages, saving lives.

AI in Education

Personalized Learning: AI tutors adapt lessons to each student's pace and style.

Access to Knowledge: Translation tools and adaptive platforms make education more inclusive.

Teacher Support: AI reduces administrative burdens, allowing educators to focus on teaching.

Example: Students in remote areas can access quality education through AI-powered online platforms.

Environmental Sustainability

Smart Systems: AI optimizes energy use in buildings, reducing waste.

Climate Modeling: AI helps scientists predict environmental changes and design solutions.

Resource Management: AI improves agriculture by monitoring soil, weather, and crop health.

Example: Farmers using AI-driven sensors can increase yields while conserving water.

Public Services and Governance

Smart Cities: AI manages traffic flow, waste collection, and energy distribution.

Fraud Detection: Governments use AI to identify irregularities in financial systems.

Citizen Engagement: AI chatbots provide faster access to public information and services.

Example: Cities deploying AI traffic systems reduce congestion and pollution, improving the quality of life.

Bridging Digital Divides

Equal Access: AI tools make technology more accessible to marginalized communities.

Empowerment: Digital skills ensure that all citizens can participate in the modern economy.

Example: AI-powered microlearning platforms help adults in underserved regions gain new skills.

Risks and Safeguards

Bias and Fairness: AI must be monitored to prevent discrimination.

Privacy: Strong safeguards are needed to protect personal data.

Ethical Use: Societies must balance innovation with responsibility.

Example: Transparent AI policies ensure that citizens benefit without sacrificing rights.

The Societal Advantage

When societies embrace AI digital skills, they unlock collective progress—healthier populations, smarter cities, sustainable environments, and more inclusive opportunities. The challenge lies in ensuring that these benefits are distributed fairly, creating a future where technology serves humanity as a whole.

CHAPTER 6

THE FUTURE OF AI SKILLS

Artificial Intelligence is evolving at a breathtaking pace. The digital skills that empower individuals and organizations today will continue to expand, reshaping the way we live, work, and interact. Preparing for this future requires not only technical knowledge but also adaptability, creativity, and foresight. This chapter explores the emerging technologies, future jobs, and strategies for building resilience in an AI-driven world.

Emerging Technologies

Generative AI: Tools that create text, images, music, and even code are redefining creativity and productivity.

Robotics: AI-powered robots will increasingly assist in manufacturing, healthcare, and domestic tasks.

Quantum Computing: Though still in its early stages, quantum AI promises breakthroughs in problem-solving and data analysis.

Example: Generative AI platforms already help architects design buildings, while future quantum systems may optimize entire cities.

Preparing for Jobs That Don't Exist Yet

Dynamic Careers: Just as social media managers and app developers emerged in the last decade, new AI-related roles will appear.

Hybrid Skills: The most valuable professionals will combine technical expertise with creativity, empathy, and ethical judgment.

Example: Future careers may include "AI ethicist," "human-AI collaboration designer," or "algorithmic auditor."

Building Resilience in a Changing World

Continuous Learning: Lifelong education will be essential as AI tools evolve.

Adaptability: Workers must be ready to pivot into new roles as industries transform.

Global Perspective: AI skills will be vital for participating in an interconnected economy.

Example: A teacher who learns to integrate AI into classrooms today is preparing students for jobs that may not yet exist.

Balancing Innovation with Humanity

Ethical Frameworks: As AI grows more powerful, societies must ensure it serves human values.

Human-Centered Design: Future AI systems should enhance human creativity and well-being, not replace them.

Example: Healthcare AI should support doctors in making better decisions, not remove the human touch from patient care.

The Road Ahead

The future of AI skills is not about mastering machines—it is about mastering collaboration with them. Those who embrace adaptability, creativity, and ethical awareness will thrive in a world where technology and humanity evolve together. The challenge is not whether AI will change the world—it already has. The challenge is whether we will be ready to shape that change for the better.

CONCLUSION

Artificial Intelligence is not a distant concept—it is the present reality shaping our lives, careers, businesses, and societies. The benefits of AI digital skills are profound: they empower individuals to thrive, enable businesses to innovate, and help societies progress toward inclusivity and sustainability. The challenge is not whether AI will change the world—it already has. The challenge is whether we will embrace the skills needed to shape that change responsibly. The future belongs to those who are prepared, adaptable, and willing to learn. By cultivating AI digital skills, we ensure that technology serves humanity, not the other way around.

REFERENCES

Bostrom, N. (2014). *Superintelligence: Paths, Dangers, Strategies.* Oxford: Oxford University Press.

Géron, A. (2019). *Hands-On Machine Learning with Scikit-Learn, Keras, and TensorFlow*. 2nd edn. Sebastopol: O'Reilly Media.

Goodfellow, I., Bengio, Y., and Courville, A. (2016). *Deep Learning.* Cambridge, MA: MIT Press.

Ng, A. (2018). *Machine Learning Yearning.* Palo Alto: Deeplearning.ai.

Shane, J. (2019). *You Look Like a Thing and I Love You: How AI Works and Why It's Making the World a Weirder Place*. New York: Little, Brown and Company.

Kissinger, H., Mundie, C., and Schmidt, E. (2023). *Genesis: Artificial Intelligence, Hope, and the Human Spirit*. New York: Little, Brown and Company.

Bender, E.M. and Hanna, A. (2024). *The AI Con: How to Fight Big Tech's Hype and Create the Future We Want*. London: Verso Books.

Witt, S. (2024). *The Thinking Machine: Jensen Huang, Nvidia, and the World's Most Coveted Microchip*. New York: Penguin Press.

Theobald, O. (2017). *Machine Learning for Absolute Beginners*. 2nd edn. North Charleston: CreateSpace Independent Publishing.

Bishop, C.M. (2006). *Pattern Recognition and Machine Learning*. New York: Springer.

Hagey, K. (2024). *The Optimist: Sam Altman, OpenAI, and the Race to Invent the Future*. New York: Crown Publishing Group.

DiCarlo, C. (2024). *Building a God: The Ethics of Artificial Intelligence and the Race to Control It*. Toronto: Humanist Press.

Mindell, D.A. (2024). *The New Lunar Society: An Enlightenment Guide to the Next Industrial Revolution.* Cambridge, MA: MIT Press.

Epps, A. (2023). *A Kids Book About AI Bias*. Portland: A Kids Book About, Inc.

FURTHER READING

Ng, A. (2018). AI for Everyone – A free online course that introduces non-technical learners to the impact of AI on business and society.

Brynjolfsson, E. and McAfee, A. (2014). The Second Machine Age – Explores how digital technologies, including AI, are reshaping economies and workplaces.

Russell, S. and Norvig, P. (2021). Artificial Intelligence: A Modern Approach – A comprehensive textbook widely used in universities for foundational AI concepts.

Haenlein, M., Kaplan, A., and Tan, C.-W. (2019). Artificial Intelligence in Business and Education – Academic articles examining AI adoption in organizational and educational contexts.

Shapiro, C. and Varian, H.R. (1999). Information Rules – Though predating modern AI, this classic explains how digital technologies transform business strategy.

Floridi, L. (2019). The Logic of Information: A Theory of Philosophy as Conceptual Design – A philosophical exploration of digital ethics and AI's role in society.

World Economic Forum (2020). Schools of the Future: Defining New Models of Education for the Fourth Industrial Revolution – A report on how AI and digital skills are reshaping education globally.

OECD (2021). AI in Society

GLOSSARY OF KEY TERMS

Artificial Intelligence (AI): The simulation of human intelligence in machines that can learn, reason, and make decisions.

Machine Learning (ML): A subset of AI where systems improve performance by learning from data rather than being explicitly programmed.

Deep Learning: A type of machine learning that uses neural networks with many layers to process complex data such as images, speech, and text.

Neural Network: A computational model inspired by the human brain, consisting of interconnected nodes ("neurons") that process information.

Natural Language Processing (NLP): AI techniques that enable machines to understand, interpret, and generate human language.

Prompt Engineering: The skill of crafting effective inputs (prompts) to guide AI systems, especially generative AI, toward useful outputs.

Data Literacy: The ability to read, understand, and work with data, including interpreting charts, statistics, and AI-driven insights.

Automation: The use of AI and technology to perform repetitive tasks with minimal human intervention.

Ethical AI: The practice of designing and using AI responsibly, ensuring fairness, transparency, privacy, and accountability.

Algorithm: A set of rules or instructions that a computer follows to solve problems or perform tasks.

Bias in AI: Systematic errors in AI outputs caused by imbalanced or prejudiced training data.

Generative AI: AI systems that can create new content—such as text, images, music, or code—based on learned patterns.

Quantum Computing: An emerging field that uses quantum mechanics to perform computations far faster than classical computers.

Digital Divide: The gap between individuals or communities who have access to digital technologies and those who do not.

AI Literacy: The ability to understand, use, and critically evaluate AI technologies in everyday life, education, and work.

FIGURES

Figure 1.1: Timeline of AI Milestones

Code

```
1956  | Dartmouth Conference – Birth of AI
1997  | IBM's Deep Blue defeats Garry Kasparov
2011  | IBM Watson wins Jeopardy!
2016  | AlphaGo defeats world champion Lee Sedol
2002  | Generative AI (ChatGPT, DALL E) enters
        mainstream
2025  | AI integrated into education, business, and
        governance
```

Figure 2.1: The AI Skills Pyramid

Code

```
Advanced Skills                 |
(AI ethics, strategy,           |
innovation leadership)          |

Intermediate Skills             |
(prompt engineering,            |
automation, collaboration)      |

Foundational Skills             |
(data literacy, digital         |
awareness, adaptability)        |
```

TABLES

Table 2.1: Comparison of Core AI Digital Skills

Skill	Description	Application Example
Data Literacy	Ability to interpret and use data	Reading dashboards, analytics
Prompt Engineering	Crafting effective inputs for AI systems	Writing queries for ChatGPT
Automation Basics	Using AI to streamline repetitive tasks	Automating reports, scheduling
Ethical Awareness	Understanding fairness, bias, and privacy	Designing responsible AI systems
Adaptability	Lifelong learning and flexibility	Upskilling in new AI tools
Collaboration with AI	Working alongside AI as a partner	AI-assisted decision-making

Table 3.1:

Skill	Description	Application Example
Data Literacy	Ability to interpret and use data	Reading dashboards, analytics
Prompt Engineering	Crafting effective inputs for AI systems	Writing queries for ChatGPT
Automation Basics	Using AI to streamline repetitive tasks	Automating reports, scheduling
Ethical Awareness	Understanding fairness, bias, and privacy	Designing responsible AI systems
Adaptability	Lifelong learning and flexibility	Upskilling in new AI tools
Collaboration with AI	Working alongside AI as a partner	AI-assisted decision-making

Table 4.1: AI Business Benefits vs. Challenges

Benefit	Challenge
Efficiency & cost savings	Workforce displacement concerns
Enhanced customer service	Data privacy risks
Innovation & insights	High implementation costs
Global competitiveness	Regulatory uncertainty
Risk management	Bias and ethical dilemmas

Table 5.1: Societal Impact of AI

Sector	Positive Impact	Risks/Concerns
Healthcare	Faster diagnosis, personalized treatment	Data privacy, misdiagnosis
Education	Personalized learning, accessibility	Over-reliance on automation
Sustainability	Smart energy, climate modeling	Tech inequality
Governance	Efficient public services	Surveillance, misuse of power